Weight Loss Motivation for Men & Women

Motivational Hacks & Strategies to Trick Your Brain and Lose Weight Fast

By Kira Novac (ISBN: 978-1-80095-030-6)

Copyright ©Kira Novac 2015

www.amazon.com/author/kira-novac

All rights reserved. No part of this publication may be reproduced, stored in a retrieval system, or transmitted, in any form or by any means, electronic, mechanical, photocopying, recording or otherwise, without the prior written permission of the author and the publishers.

The scanning, uploading, and distribution of this book via the Internet, or via any other means, without the permission of the author is illegal and punishable by law. Please purchase only authorized electronic editions, and do not participate in or encourage electronic piracy of copyrighted materials.

All information in this book has been carefully researched and checked for factual accuracy. However, the author and publishers make no warranty, expressed or implied, that the information contained herein is appropriate for every individual, situation or purpose, and assume no responsibility for errors or omission. The reader assumes the risk and full responsibility for all actions, and the author will not be held liable for any loss or damage, whether consequential, incidental, and special or otherwise, that may result from the information presented in this publication.

A physician has not written the information in this book. Before making any serious dietary changes, I advise you to consult with your physician first.

A free eBook edition is availabe with the purchase of this book

Free eBook Link (Kindle edition):

http://bit.ly/weight-loss-motivation-book

Table of contents

About the Book 1
   Your Weight Loss Journey Made Exciting and Fun 1
   What you'll learn in this book 5

Introduction 8

Chapter 1-Slim DOWN or what?! Why we need to lose weight?... 34
   Risks to health – and health is wealth 34
   Physical fitness 35
   Get Noticed, The Good Way 35
   Slim Body Equals Fatter Wallet 38

Chapter 2-May the motivation be with you – but how? 41
   Slow and steady wins the race 41
   Introduce some excitement! 43
   Start cleaning out your closet 45
   Come up with a proper plan 47
   Reward yourself 51
   Include a friend 53
   Get a personal trainer 55

Chapter 3-Why can't I stick to the plan? 57
   The "I can't do it" 57
   The "What if I fail?" 60
   The "I don't want to do it" 63
   The "What if I succeed?" 66
   The "It wasn't supposed to be this hard" 68

Chapter 4-No Guilt Trips – What to do when you get off track 71

Let yourself off easy!..71
Jog your memory, remember the purpose! 74
Set small scale goals for yourself..77
Honesty time – what are my weaknesses?.................................. 78
Conclusion... 81
To post an honest review 82

About the Book

Your Weight Loss Journey Made Exciting and Fun

When one plans to go on a weight loss plan, for whatever reasons and encompassing whatever activities, it is not very difficult for one to start. You can find tons of articles on the internet, explaining how to start on a weight loss plan, how to make a proper schedule, what things to do, and what to avoid, etc. But a topic that is rarely addressed anywhere is how to stick to a weight loss plan, and more importantly, what to do when you find yourself getting sidetracked. It's not only about information. You also need inspiration and motivation to keep on track. As a weight loss and health coach, very often I get asked about motivation and creating new habits. Most of my clients know that eating a healthy diet pays off. They know physical fitness makes sense. They just need more motivation. I have been there myself. I am not judging. Instead, I want to teach you some practical and doable solutions, so you get awesome results fast. Your success is my success. I love assisting people in all kinds of transformations. I want to help you, so you don't feel frustrated but keep taking meaningful and purposeful action with a sense of excitement and a clearly defined vision. After reading this book, you will know how, and your motivation will be automatic. You will also learn how to draw motivation from different sources, so there is always something to fall back on, even when you have a bad day (we all have those, right? Nobody is perfect!).

Rule number one is- no guilt-trips. No matter what happens, always remember self-guilt is a poison, and you need to approach all kinds of failures and getting off track with a sense of self-love, as well as self-humor. This book is a non-judgment, fluff-free guide for all men and women who want to get and stay motivated like they deserve. Throughout the book, I don't want to call myself a mentor or a guru. Instead, I want to be your friend and offer a simple step-by-step walk-through. Always remember to take action, apply even the simplest strategies I suggest, test them, and only then, move on to trying something new. During my weight loss journey and also prior to writing this book, I have devoured dozens, if not hundreds, of motivational resources. I have finally learned that the information I gathered from all of them was pretty much the same. There is not too much new motivational stuff that can really be created. However, what was always different was me- my way of thinking, my transformation, and my journey. I learned that the most important thing to actually succeed with weight loss is not how much you know or how much information you gather, but how much you apply and test.

This is why I am writing this book. I want to show you what worked for me and what I apply on a daily basis, not only to maintain my healthy weight, but also to keep positive and motivated in other areas of my life.

My message for you- you are special and so is your journey. If you have already read books on motivation and self-help, you have probably noticed there are two kinds, or they all have two kinds of messages.

The first kind of motivational material has one goal. It wants to make you feel good about yourself so you leave the world of self-guilt, destructive habits (poor nutrition and lack of physical activity are some of them, and so is drinking or smoking) and embrace the world of self-love instead. I like this approach, and I think it works well for most people, including myself.

The second kind of motivational material is a tough love, kind of "move your ass now" dynamic stuff. It tries to use pain and negative emotions to help you take action and get more mental toughness (nobody will cry for you, go to the gym now, and stop feeling sorry for yourself, be responsible, and don't eat that crap!). Honestly, I think this approach may work for some individuals, and I have nothing against it, but everyone is different. It means everyone works differently in terms of feeding our minds with motivational books or programs. Before embarking on your journey, you need to ask yourself whether you prefer a gentle approach or maybe the tough love one. I think both are great, but the common mistake that many motivational programs make (this is my personal opinion) is that they stick too much to just one approach.

This is why I decided to apply both of them, so you have the freedom to choose whatever works for you. I will respect all your choices. You don't have to apply all the strategies I suggest in this book. You can just pick one and stick to it. Changes are better made step by step. Don't try to take on way too much all at once.

What you'll learn in this book

- Why you should lose weight in the first place, and why weight loss is only the tip of the iceberg
- Motivational tips and tricks to stay on track of your weight loss plan and keep yourself from slacking, plus follow up plans if you have a bad day (because it's OK to have a bad day)
- Process vs Results and Progress vs. Perfection
- Why society has brainwashed us into thinking we can't do it and that it's "easier" for us to remain fat and unfit.
- Some of the major reasons you find yourself slacking on the plan; find your WHY so you can get to the root of the problem
- How to counter factors of demotivation and hopelessness and prevent them from affecting your routine
- Excellent and practical tips on how to get back on track with your weight loss plan if you find yourself slacking.
- Practical suggestions to always make sure you have some healthy food and meals and are always ready to move your body to feel and look amazing!

So what are you waiting for? This book will tell you all about what you need to do to not let the momentary lapse in determination get to you, and instead, get back on track with renewed vigor and enthusiasm!

Let the journey begin,

Kira Novac

Free Complimentary Recipe eBook

Thank you so much for taking an interest in my work!
As a thank you, I would love to offer you a free complimentary recipe eBook to help you achieve vibrant health. It will teach you how to prepare amazingly tasty and healthy detox smoothies so that you never feel deprived or bored again!

Download your free eBook here:

http://detox.kiraglutenfreerecipes.com

Introduction

Before we jump into the ocean of motivation, let me tell you this short story.

Susan goes shopping, and she bumps into an old friend of hers, Mary, back from college.

Mary had been severely overweight at that time, but now she has slimmed down so much that Susan hardly recognized her. Mary looks like a model now, and she seems to be full of energy!

"Wow, Mary!" said Susan. "You look fantastic! What have you done to lose so much weight? Congratulations!"

###

This is a normal reaction, right? You would probably say and ask the same. Most people would (well some people might skip the "congrats" part or just say it with no deeper meaning, but that's a topic for another book actually. We always need to remember to get inspired and motivated by other people's success. It will help you on your journey!).

Then, Susan drives back home. She can see her neighbor doing some jogging while she's driving. The following day, she is at work. While she and most of her colleagues choose to go out for some crappy fast food for lunch, one of her colleagues, Bob, chooses to stay in and eat his healthy lunch and a salad. Everyone just leaves, and nobody cares about Bob and his salad, just like nobody really cares about Susan's neighbor jogging.

Do you see a problem with that? I do! You see, our society congratulates people on fast results, but nobody (or very few people) congratulates people on going to the gym or gradually shifting their diet in a more natural, wholesome, and healthy direction.

Think about it. You are taking a very important step as you want to lose weight. You are sick and tired of your current weight, and so you go on Amazon or some other platform and get this book and maybe some other books as well. In other words, you begin to go through a process. You know you need more motivation, and you take action. You are one step closer to achieving your goal. But very few people will congratulate you on taking this step. Maybe I will be the only one congratulating you on this super important step, and I will also congratulate you on cooking a healthy recipe tomorrow and maybe joining the gym this week. But most people won't. Why?

Because people want fast results, but they skip the importance of process.

If you see that there is nobody congratulating you for each and every step (aside from your friend Kira and maybe a few other people who support you), you will need to congratulate yourself. This is called self-love. You will need to learn to embrace and enjoy the process of your weight loss journey. It's all about creating healthy rituals that very few people will actually see. They will get curious though, when they start seeing the results. Then, they will ask you for the magic pill. What's the magic pill?

The process.

Think about it. There are many technologies that help people lose weight. Take liposuction for example. You can pay through the nose and get instant results. This is what most people want, but then give it a few months, and they put the weight back on, as they haven't mastered the process of creating healthy habits. Personally, to me, it doesn't make any sense. Having the right mindset is the key to success, and we always need to ask ourselves questions to get to the root of the problem.

If you are asking yourself any of the following questions, cheer up as I have all the answers. Moreover, I have been there myself, and I know how it feels. The weight loss journey can be tough if you lack motivation and support.

So, the questions you may have are:

- *Diets suck, as I will have to starve. So how can I stick to something I hate?*
- *Gym is boring as heck; I hate it. Can I still lose weight?*
- *I love socializing with people and eating good food. I want to lose weight but come on! I don't want to give up on socializing!*
- *I have tried to lose weight many times and I always failed. My friends must think I am a loser. Is it worth trying again? What if I fail?*
- *Honestly, I really want to lose weight, but all my family and friends are overweight. What if I lose weight, and then I lose them, or they get jealous of my health success?*

Here's one thing to understand. Those questions are usually either excuses or limiting beliefs. You see, we need to learn how to <u>trick our brain,</u> because our brain's only function is to keep us alive and in our comfort zone. However, to lose weight, we need to leave our comfort zone and adapt new habits. We need to accept the fact that we may fall victim to either our own excuses or limiting beliefs. In both cases, our brain is to blame. And very often, our brain is programmed by our family and friends, as we get many limiting beliefs from them. It's not that our close ones don't want us to succeed with our goals, in this particular case, weight loss. It's just they are either scared themselves or simply want to keep us safe (what if the weight loss program you pick is a scam, and you lose your money not your weight?). Sound familiar?

Let's have a look at some of the common excuses and limiting beliefs and how to overcome them:

Old belief: Diets are boring, and you have to go hungry.

New belief: healthy eating is fun, and you can enjoy good, healthy food without feeling deprived. It all comes down to regularly educating oneself, getting and trying new healthy recipes, and substituting some unhealthy ingredients with their healthier counterparts. It's easy if you put your mind to it. Besides, it's not only about weight loss. We want to invest in our health, so we can still have a blast at our grandchildren's weddings, right?

Remember, it's not about eating less, you have to eat right. Feed your body with nutrient-dense foods. Yes, at first, stuff like chia seeds, quinoa, spirulina or other healthy food may seem weird, or you may even reject it as "odd food," but eventually, you will learn how to create tasty and healthy meals with those and other "weird" ingredients, and it will all become automatic. Focus on the process.

Old belief: Gym is boring as heck; I hate it. Can I still lose weight?

New belief: everything can be viewed as boring. It depends on your focus and your mindset. You know that physical activity is crucial, not only for weight loss, but also for staying fit and feeling great. It's so much better than taking medications for stress, anxiety, and other common 21st century diseases that all have roots in stress. Get to the root of the problem, move your body, and improve your emotional wellbeing as well.

Here is what has helped me overcome my anti-gym attitude:

- I told myself the reason I go to the gym is to feel good and leave all the stress there, and I stopped obsessing about how I looked and that I was still overweight. Everyone has to start somewhere, right? Trying and failing is better than not taking action.

- I got committed to re-committing. I told myself it's OK to get off track sometimes and re-committing myself to my fitness plan forms part of my journey
- I created really awesome playlists with my favorite songs, songs that would give me lots of positive energy and make me feel good. Whenever I felt like not going to the gym, I would just play the songs at home and start jumping and dancing to them. This would always end up in a workout!
- I convinced 2 other women from my neighborhood (they also wanted to lose weight) to join the gym with me. We would all go together in the car (less gas bill right?) 2, sometimes, 3 times a week. We had a very detailed plan of doing exercise first and then jumping into the pool and Jacuzzi and steam room. Then, we would pamper ourselves and go for a nice meal at a whole foods restaurant or at our homes (we would rotate our cooking shifts). This is how we stayed motivated to keep learning and cooking new healthy recipes. By treating ourselves to occasional healthy meals out, we knew we had to deserve it. It would also give us more ideas, as we loved the menu at our local healthy restaurant.
- I always had a plan B in the form of fitness DVD's that I would exercise to when, for some reason, I did not want to go to the gym. It worked fantastically, because there was more variety in my workouts, and I did not feel bored with the gym like I used to.

- I devised a very smart plan to combine workout with cleaning my house. I'm not too sure if men can do it; it's usually women who are better at multi-tasking, but I guess everyone can give it a try. I would squeeze a series of squats, stretches and other simple sets of short fitness activities in between vacuum cleaning, mopping, and doing the dishes. After everything was done, I would pamper myself in an aromatherapy bath and meditate or do yoga. Then, when the kids were back from school, I felt fantastic, as I had done my stuff (moms need to do their own stuff as well, right?), plus the house was nice and clean. It really feels great when there is no stress, you know you have done your workout, your cleaning and other house chores, and you can finally spend time with your loved ones. I like the fact that I no longer felt stressed-out or exhausted. In the evenings, I would go for a walk with my husband and kids and plan healthy meals and see friends. Of course, you need to figure out what works for your schedule, but if you are a stay at home mom, or a freelancer working from home like I am, this strategy could help me. And don't forget about the music that will keep you going! If you are working in a full-time job, consider getting up a bit earlier so that you can do your workout first thing in the morning. You will feel so much better (and more energized) at work. Start small. If your usual wake-up and get-up time is, let's say 7AM, start getting up at 6:45 and go from there.

Ok, back to limiting beliefs that only kill your motivation.

Old beliefs: it's actually 3 limiting beliefs in 1. (I put them all together as they are kind of related)

- *I love socializing with people and eating good food. I want to lose weight but come on! I don't want to give up socializing!*
- *I have tried to lose weight many times, and I always failed. My friends must think I am a loser. Is it worth trying again? What if I fail?*
- *Honestly, I really want to lose weight, but all my family and friends are overweight. What if I lose weight, and then I lose them, or they get jealous of my health success?*

New belief: You can still socialize when on a weight loss journey. You just need to make sure you have a clear enough vision and let everyone around you know about it. You could also try to convince them to join you. Simply tell them you are not going on the latest fad diet, but you feel sick and tired of feeling sick and tired. You are an adult, and you want to be responsible for your own health. Let them know you want to learn more about nutrition, so you can take care of both your health and taste buds at the same time. Add that you respect their choices, even though you don't make them anymore, and you prefer healthy food. This is why they should respect yours.

Another option would be to master some recipes that are both healthy and tasty. It's not that you have to survive on salads alone. You can also learn to make some healthy, sugar-free muffins or cakes. It doesn't take long to learn new recipes. Learn them and have everyone love you for it!

Also, don't fear that people will not like you anymore when they see your health and wellness success. Instead, see it as your obligation and use it for more motivation. The healthier you get, the more you can help other people. This is what really motivates me to live healthy. I love sharing my transformation and practical, healthy living tools that modern families can apply. Of course, there are always some people who gossip and criticize, but who cares? I prefer to focus on people who support us and help us. I also want to help them.

One more tip- it's good to surround yourself with people who have similar health and weight loss goals. I met my gym buddies via meetup.com. Otherwise, I would have gotten off track for good! Aside from weight loss motivation, I was also able to help them (we got committed to motivating one another). But we also became good friends, and now, our kids play together, we do vacation trips together and create really amazing moments.

You can do it now. Go to meetup.com and create your local weight loss motivation mastermind. Otherwise, it can be a pretty lonely journey. Sure, everyone wants to lose weight, but very few people commit to it, and you don't want to be among wishers but amongst doers. Another option is to go online and search for Facebook or Google + groups. However, in my case, what really worked was creating a local group offline. The dangers with online groups is you may end up spending way too much time in front of your PC or other devices, and if you want to lose weight, your number one goal should be to move your body. Go out. Leave the freaking house. Whether it's walking, biking, running or going to the gym, the success starts when you put on your workout clothes and shoes and leave the house. That's my point.

Source of Motivation

How many times has it happened that one incident or another took place, which forced you to think about trimming the fat? You know, start losing some weight and become physically fit, and if we may, become generally more acceptable in society's eyes. The incidents that you forced you to think along these lines could be anything, really: a friend's goading at a party, a pair of awesome jeans you came across while window shopping at the mall and regretfully resigning yourself to the fact you won't be able to fit in them, the desire to be physically fit and active, or any other. While people are generally different, most of us would eventually give in to the continuously arising temptations and vow to start on a weight loss plan.

In my case, it was quite simple. I was in constant physical pain, inflammation, and insecurity, and I felt no energy and no zest for life. I knew I had to change something. I remember one day, I drove my son to school, and I was hanging out near the playground talking to other moms. I suddenly heard some older kids (probably early teens- eleven or twelve) laughing at my ass. They said: "OMG! This is a really fat cow!"

I felt really embarrassed, as almost everyone near me could hear it, and it also happened that I was the only fat person there. Other moms were always so perfect and so beautiful. I was always thinking: "Wow, if I wasn't so tired, maybe I could also be more active and lose weight." However, I would always postpone it.

In the past, I would blame other people and circumstances. It was either my pregnancy or anti-depressants I was taking during a not that light period of my life. Then, as a stay-at-home mom, all my attention was on my family and cooking traditional family meals for them. Then, even though I thought I was eating a healthy diet, more and more convenience meals would enter our kitchen. Vicious cycle.

Now, I don't want to bore you with my story. But I want to share it, as there is a lesson to learn. Sometimes, we all need a kick in the ass (just like I said in the beginning, there are two kinds of motivational materials, right?). For me, it was those nasty kids who would laugh at me. I felt humiliated. Very humiliated. I still remember driving back home and crying, but I decided to use it to my advantage. I said: "enough." Enough of that. I am going to do the best I can to lose weight. I need to learn how to live a healthy lifestyle. Not only did I want to lose weight, but I also wanted more energy to be a good mom, wife and friend. Not to mention, at that time, I wanted to start my business, and I was still waiting for the right moment (I did not have energy or inspiration).

I am grateful for that day. Really grateful. It forced me to transform my body and my life. Now, I feel blessed to be a holistic nutritionist, recipe writer, and weight loss coach, helping other men and women achieve their health goals as well. I am not saying this to brag, and I don't want to sound pompous. But I want to assure you that you can create the body that you want. Your MIND is stronger than you believe. This book will show you how to use it to your advantage and how to control it, rather than have it control you.

In the past, I lacked focus and consistency. I would sign up for the gym only to do one aerobics class and give up (because I felt too fat, or I felt insulted as some fit guys or gals would scan me up and down). I was the first one to buy weight loss diets, a program's magic pills, and who knows what. I spent thousands of dollars on coaches. Many of them were awesome, but I was stupid enough to think that just "hiring" them would do the job, and so again, Kira did not take action! Then I would blame the coach and stop showing up, only to purchase the next hot deal (yes, in 4 easy to pay installments of $ 99.9!).

So what happened the day those nasty kids started laughing at me and my body?

I suddenly felt compelled to take action. It was a mix of anger, sadness, and frustration that helped me take the first and most important step. I drove back home, changed, put my fitness clothes and running shoes on, and I just went out for a run. Suddenly, it did not matter that it was a cold day during late fall. Suddenly, I did not think about the workout sequence from the latest fitness program and how I looked. I just went for it.

Lesson to learn:

Most of us already know what's healthy. Most of us know how to walk and run. Most of us know that simply adding more fresh fruits and vegetables into our diets, while eliminating processed crap, and learning to cook healthy, family-friendly recipes will help us lose weight while keeping our bellies happy. We all know this stuff. So why do humans always wait to purchase the latest new stuff, whether it's a diet or workout program?

Don't get me wrong. Learning new things about healthy living is always great, and I do recommend all kinds of research. But sometimes, we use it as a shield, and we don't take action. We keep gaining information, and we never apply it.

Does it ring a bell?

- How many calories does it have?
- How many squats shall I do?
- OMG, I got off track. I hate myself. I will never lose weight.
- Is it alkaline enough?
- Is it paleo enough?
- What is the best diet to lose weight?

Answer- the best diet is called a healthy lifestyle, and it always depends on the person. Some people will do better on a paleo diet, and some people will do better on vegan or vegetarian diets, just like some people can't tolerate gluten! Everyone is different. Now, this is not a book on health or diets, so let's focus back on motivation. The thing is, you will never find out "the best diet" unless you try it and create it for yourself. The best thing you can do is take yourself out of the diet mindset and join the healthy lifestyle mindset.

The word diet is something we usually associate with deprivation, and we don't want to feel deprived, right?

The word Lifestyle, on the other hand, brings in some more positive associations, for example, abundance. Healthy lifestyle of abundance! I like it. What about you? Please let me know in the review section of this book.

You see, that day when I got laughed at, I just made a decision. I decided to create health and be slim. I got back from my run, had a shower, and I immediately googled healthy dinner recipes. I looked up the first recipe I found online, printed it, went shopping, got back and cooked it. I remember it was chicken with veggies and quinoa. I also made a salad. I told my husband I needed to change my lifestyle and lose weight. He looked at me saying: "Did you get another program again?" I said: "No, this time I will follow the common sense approach!"

Not long after that, our son was diagnosed with celiac disease, and we all switched to a gluten-free diet. This was another motivator on my journey. We all care about our family and their health, right? Even if you are single, think about it. You need energy and vibrant health, so you can create a career you want and feel great in your body, so when the time is right for you, you can start a family and be healthy enough to be there for them. It's not only about making money, just like it's not only about weight loss. **Creating health should be your priority.** With health, you feel more positive and energetic, so you can move your body and, consequently, lose more weight without over worrying or over stressing out. Also, with more health, you can invest more time and effort in your professional life.

Lesson I learned:

Put health before weight loss. Pick up the first thing you know (maybe a healthy recipe or a quick power walk), and do it now. You can even pause reading this book for half an hour. Just pick up one thing you know is good for you and your health. Take a break from reading. This is what I did on my breakthrough day. What is your breakthrough day? Is it today? Celebrate it by doing something healthy!

MAKE THE DECISION. IT HAS TO BE NOW OR NEVER.

ARE YOU READY? ARE YOU WITH ME?

DO YOU WANT TO TRANSFORM YOUR BODY AND MIND?

Of course, getting started is one thing. But, once people start on a weight loss plan, they realize that along with the various sacrifices, and the new and much harder routine, to which they have to adjust their bodies, there's another factor that is just as crucial and difficult- how to stick to the routine. This is one of the lesser-addressed issues you won't find so readily available on the internet or in the library. And it has happened countless times that people get started on a weight loss plan with all the essentials, but they don't know how to remain motivated enough to continue after a certain amount of time. They don't see the results fast enough, and so they quit. Tough nut to crack! I have been there. The solution is not that complicated though:

- Always congratulate yourself for each baby step taken; you don't need to wait to lose weight to be happy. You can be happy right now, so you can happily achieve your weight loss goals.
- Celebrate all those tiny steps.
- Accept failure as a part of success. Most people are not able to stick to a weight loss program or a diet in a 100% perfect way. In fact, I would venture to say that nobody does (maybe you can find an exception; if so, please let me know. I'd be curious to hear about it). Remember, you can always re-commit, and it's also OK to get off track if you can get right back on it. Remember the story I mentioned right at the

beginning? Whenever you feel sad, frustrated, or unmotivated, remind yourself of the following:

Forget about perfection. Go for progress. It's always those little things.

Attract your motivation and your vision to the process of progress. Do not get too fixated on perfection or impeccable results. If you get off track, for example, you indulge in sweets or something you were not supposed to eat, don't beat yourself up. Make up for it by doing something healthy. Go for a walk, do a series of squats (By the way, ladies, squats are a real game changer, so get started now!) and move forward.

Your time should not be wasted focusing on what you have done wrong. Allow yourself some small margins to fail. With this attitude, you will feel happier and more emotionally free. This will help you feel better, healthier, and make healthier choices. Do not act from the point of restriction, self-anger, and self-guilt. If you feel those moments approaching (and again nobody is perfect), make sure you listen to something positive. I always have some inspirational audios on self-love and positive thinking in my car and on my phone. I call it a diet for my mind and emotions. While, on a physical level, I aim to eat healthy food and move my body, I also nourish my mind soul and emotions. I am loving it!

Because a real, **holistic weight loss plan** does not only entail a physical aspect (diet, workout), but rather a mental and emotional aspect as well, and both are equally important if one wants to stick to the plan and see it through!

Along with this, we shall focus on another important aspect below, understanding the problem. Whenever we are faced with any sort of problem or situation in life we have to solve, you might find the following quote resonating through your brain: Half the solution lies in understanding the problem. It is quite true; before you move on to solving a problem, you have to understand what the problem actually is, the various factors involved, the potential risks you might come across, and how to avoid them. As soon as you have your why, you will have your how.

Grab a piece of paper and a pen and try to come up with at least 5 reasons (or more) why you want to lose weight. Be sure to think of all areas of your life and how they will be positively affected if you manage to lose weight.

Yes, I know; I can hear some surprised voices: But Kira! 5 reasons are a lot! I am not as creative as you are.

Well yea, it may seem like a lot, but trust me, as soon as you start writing, you will come up with more than 10. Also, it's not about creativity; it's about listening to your heart. Repeat the process whenever you feel sad or unmotivated. Keep the list with you at all times. I felt OK to share it with my husband, and I had no problem having my list of WHYs all around the house (kitchen, bathroom, closet, I even had it on my front door in case I wanted to go out and grab some sweets. My WHYs would serve as a reminder, and so I would go back to kitchen and make myself a healthy smoothie with coconut oil and pure cocoa).

By the way, if you crave sugar, have a tablespoon of coconut oil. It really does the trick.

Back to your why's. Create the list now. You can thank me later.

Let me share my list with you. I still have it in my office and in my car. Even though I am happy with my weight now, I use it as a reminder to keep on the healthy track and help other people. Trust me, it's not easy to share all my reasons with my readers, but I know this can help you, so there we go!

I want to lose weight, and I deserve to lose weight and transform my body, because:

1. I want to create a healthy, fit body that inspires other people for healthy living.
2. With a healthy and slim body, I will feel more confident in all areas of my life.
3. I will have more energy and zest for life, and I will no longer feel depressed.
4. I will learn all about healthy foods and healthy recipes, so that I can take care of my family and be a better mom and wife.
5. I want to become a holistic nutritionist. I need to create a healthy lifestyle first. I need to help myself so that I can help other people.
6. I want to start my own business. If I don't lose weight, and if I don't have more energy, it will never happen.
7. I want to wear exactly what I want and whenever I want.
8. I want my kids to be proud of me.
9. I want to protect myself from cancer and other diseases. This is why I need to take care of my health.

10. I want to travel and keep learning new things. I need more energy and health.

As you can see, some of my WHY's were egoistic (I want to wear what I want and when I want), but some were more inspired by my desire to help other people. It's good to have different ways to get motivated. There were days when I did not feel like doing anything, but I looked at my WHY's, and I reminded myself that I want to take care of my family' health and inspire them. Another day, I would browse through fashion magazines and imagine myself wearing my dream bikini.

The bottom line is, all WHY's are awesome.

Now brainstorm and come up with yours.

Finally, I'll leave this quote here to act as an initial source of motivation to keep you going. Write it down and keep it in your office, car, and wallet; stick it on your fridge and bathroom mirror and let it soak into your sub conscious:

One of the greatest moments in life is realizing that two weeks ago, your body couldn't have done what it just did.

I believe in YOU. Now, you need to believe in yourself as well.

Accept yourself the way you are now. Approach everything you do with excitement. Instead of being angry with yourself, always laugh and face challenges with a sense of humor. We all make mistakes, and society is constantly bombarding us with the image of perfection. But we need to learn to celebrate the process.

Remember what I told you. I recommend before moving on to the next chapter, you do something healthy. Maybe you can make a smoothie? Or pick up a new healthy recipe (don't overstress about calories though), or maybe grab your phone or MP3 player (make sure you have your favorite music in there), and go for a walk. Whatever it is that you do, smile. I know it sounds stupid and childish, but smiling will help you feel good. Besides, it's free, and it looks great on you!

Chapter 1-Slim DOWN or what?! Why we need to lose weight?

Risks to health – and health is wealth

Like we have previously concluded, looking slim and fit aren't the only reasons people look to lose weight. Many people try to trim down in order to avoid a multitude of diseases. Yes, that's plural! Being overweight isn't something that's just bad for the looks, it can also cause all sorts of serious health problems – both physical and mental. Being overweight can lead to problems of the heart, as well as higher blood pressure. It can result in some certain types of cancer, diabetes, strokes and back pain. Being overweight can also lead to depression (I have been there myself).

As the famous saying goes, health is wealth. It's sad how most of us never realize the painful truth of this saying until it's too late. Let's make a pledge not to be among those people, and start focusing on our health and healthy weight loss.

Physical fitness

Attaining physical fitness can do more than just give you good looks, and even make you a center of attention at some places. It also does wonder for your health. As stated above, health is wealth, we won't elaborate on that. Moreover, you'll find yourself more active throughout the day, and more effective and efficient in all the tasks you'll tackle! Physical fitness also means greater sex life and it actually acts as a natural anti-age treatment.

Get Noticed, The Good Way

I don't mean to be offensive, but you know how in a crowd, the person (or persons) who stand out are those who are overweight? This is why some nasty kids laughed at me when I was fat. I was the only one. I was the fattest.

It's sad but this is what us, humans do. It's like your eye is automatically drawn to them, though you try to look away when you catch them looking your way. And some people don't even bother to do that, and it just becomes really uncomfortable when people are staring. If you've never been on the receiving end of such stares, reading about it and imagining it could hardly make it any exciting. There are two things you can do.

1. Stay where you are and choose to be a victim. All people around you are bad and so you choose to comfort yourself with some crappy food and a healthy diet can wait for better times (I had been there myself many times and so I am not judging).
2. Use it as your motivator and take massive action. This is what I did. I thought: what? Some stupid kids making fun of me? I was angry as heck. My anger got me started actually. If I ever see those kids, I will thank them (plus I will tell their parents to teach them good manners too).

If you lose weight, you still have a chance to get noticed, only, not the bad way. Imagine the scenario: you are overweight, and one day you decide that you've just had enough. You go on an intense 'I wanna lose weight' mission, which can encompass both dieting, eating healthy foods (which may even contain some of those vegetables you've always hated, but hey, such is the level of your determination) and exercising. You stick to the plan rigorously, not allowing yourself to slack or anything. Even if you have a bad day and get off track, you manage to get up, brush yourself off and get back on track. The game is not over! A couple of months' later swings by the annual family dinner at your parents' house. You go to it, and you're the center of attention! That's not saying much since you always were, but the bad way. Having to smile uncomfortably through all the jeers and laughter directed at your weight. Well, not anymore! Now you can look those people in the eye, match their dumbfounded stares with a winning smile, then smirk and walk away.

"How did you do it?"

First, they think you are weird as you are all about eating weird, healthy foods and you work out 5 days a week. Then, they see the results and they "wanna know how". You tell them about your process. Plus, you tell them that now you are a health and fitness nut and that you love it so much that it has become your lifestyle. This is how you inspire your family and friends to take better care of themselves. It feels great if you can help those around you.

Sounds wonderful, doesn't it? We've made our point.

Slim Body Equals Fatter Wallet

While not a universal principle, it is generally true that a man's wallet and his weight have an inversely proportional relationship. It's no secret that overweight people love to eat and are ready to sacrifice a sizeable portion of their income – or pocket money – on food without a second thought. While I don't mean to judge them on this (I have been there myself) and certainly such people are invaluably awesome when you have a date and don't know any new good places to go eat, the fact remains that well, think of all you could do with the money you could save by like, not spending that much on food (especially expensive take away or eating out).

When you go on a diet, you spend less on eating out as the first stage is mostly about creating your healthy weight loss foundation. I really recommend you start eating at home and get committed to batch-cooking. That also equals saving money! Cook in batches and freeze your food.

That means no more processed ice cream or French fries and soft drinks– or as much as you used to have anyway. Instead, you'll find yourself settling for vegetables and healthy foods. You can make your own ice cream at home (dairy free option like coconut milk and almond milk work great for that). While that may not sound very exciting, remind yourself of what you get out of it. Remember the awesome family trip you been dreaming about for months? Or maybe some new clothes (perfect for your new awesome weight!). Well, you can have that not remain a dream anymore.

Some people may disagree by saying that healthy foods are expensive. This is what I used to think myself. However, by shopping in bulk and getting coupon codes, as well as planning your meals in advance and cooking in batches, you will be able to save up lots of money and time and get more health and energy. Weight loss is an added bonus. When you eat healthy, nutrient-dense foods, you are able to feed your body with what it needs. This is why you actually end up eating less. Usually people overeat because of 2 factors:

1. They eat too much processed foods that are high in calories and low in nutrients. Since there are no nutrients, our body feels hungry all the time. And so it craves more processed foods and we end up in a vicious cycle.
   Solution- focus on adding more nutrients into your diet. I am not talking about vitamin pills but real foods with real nutrients that you and your beautiful body deserve.
2. They eat because they are bored or stressed out. This was my problem. I was an emotional eater.

Solution- whenever you feel tempted to eat only to fight stress, try to relax first. Take a few deep breaths. Stretch your body. Get involved in natural, holistic relaxation techniques like for example yoga, meditation or mindfulness. The more you master relaxation, the more control you will have to change your relationship with food. You have the power to control how you feel.

Chapter 2-May the motivation be with you – but how?

Slow and steady wins the race

Remember the story we read back in childhood, of the race between a rabbit and a turtle? Yeah, what was the moral of it? Slow and steady wins the race.

That moral comes in quite handy when you go on a mission to lose weight. The girl or a guy you like called you fat, and after the initial depression phase, you find yourself filled with humiliation and fury; you'll show her/him! And so you go on an intense diet plan that is not sustainable and can be bad for your health; you won't eat breakfast at all, or dinner. Just a light lunch will do, that too of only vegetables, and maybe a fruit in the evening. Bad news? That won't do. You have your motivation but your strategy is not the best one. You'll just be risking your health, and probably find yourself in the hospital, on drips, before the second day of your mission.

The point of this little scary anecdote is that when you start out big and perfect and with more passion than sense, chances are you'll flat on your face. One of the biggest causes of giving up on a diet plan is when you start out too big and soon find out that you can't stick to it.

We have already stated that it's not that much about eating less- it's about eating right. Avoid the mistake of going on a starvation diet.

The proper way to start losing weight is to start *out* with a simple plan. Yes, simple, nothing too complicated. Start by adding more fruits and vegetables. Whenever having sugar cravings, have a healthy smoothie. First focus on adding more whole some foods so that you are able to commit yourself to reducing your unhealthy dietary habits gradually, and starting out with a couple of exercises. Once you're comfortable with your new routine both mentally and physically, then slowly start improving the diet and increasing the exercises. That way, it'll be a lot easier to stick to the plan. Baby steps. The biggest mistake that people make is to try to do it all at once. But a person coming from a world of processed foods and hamburgers may kind of find it hard to become a raw food vegan in less than 2 days (unless they do it for spiritual reasons which is a topic for another book).

Introduce some excitement!

Let's face it, the process of losing weight is no fun when you first get started. While the end result may be very desirable, what you have to go through to get there is always quite arduous – kind of like studying. The key here is to make the process of losing weight more enjoyable, something you actually look forward to. That way, not only will you find it easier to stick to the plan, but also doing so with more dedication. How to become passionate about weight loss?

Here are a couple of things you can try. If going on a walk or jog is part of your plan, try doing that with a friend. It can be anyone really, be it a family member, or a neighbor, or someone from your office or school. Just make sure it isn't anyone you dislike! That way, you'll have some company, and you'll look forward to the task. You will also have someone to egg you on or persuade you out of your laziness when feel skipping a day.

Similarly, if you have a workout session as part of your plan, you can get yourself some good speaker or headphones, and put on your favorite music as you work out! A nice tip we would give here which has proved particularly helpful for a lot of people goes thus: You know the dramatic and inspirational soundtracks in movies?

Especially action movies. Add some of those to your playlist. That way, along with chick songs or whatever you have on your playlist, you'll have some tracks which will motivate you into doing that extra push-up.

Set small goals and reward yourself after achieving them. What are small goals?

For example: go for a run, or a swim or join a Zumba class and then reward myself with new fitness clothes, or watch my favorite TV show, or go to the cinema. You don't have to wait till you achieve your perfect weight- you can congratulate yourself for taking consistent action. It's always those little things.

Start cleaning out your closet

This isn't something which might be very obvious at first. What, are we suggesting cleaning out the closet as part of some exercise? Is that even an exercise? That hardly sounds any helpful, to be honest. Is this just a ruse to make you clean out OUR closets?

Nothing of that sort. Once you start out on your program of losing weight, and after sticking to it for a specific amount of time start seeing the much-desired changes in yourself, that is the perfect moment to stick a nail in the coffin in the perpetuity of your new routine. Get rid of your previous clothes, the ones that used to fit you in the old days but now just hang loosely on you. Give them to charity, sell them on a garage sale, or maybe burn them if they serve as a bad memory. Replace them with new clothes, clothes that fit the new you. This way, anytime you find yourself going off track and gaining weight again, the fact that you don't have any clothes that will fit you if you grow beyond a certain point will serve as a pretty strong motivation to get back on track.

Sounds kind of simple, but effective!

This is the best moment of the journey. As a female, I would also suggest getting a new haircut or something. Start a new chapter in your life. Start meeting new people. Start going out and dancing. Keep re-enforcing your new beliefs and lifestyle with positive affirmations:

- I control how I feel
- I love taking my health to the next level
- I am a health and fitness nut- it's just who I am
- I love healthy food
- I love working out to make my body stronger

At the same time, take on something more challenging. Maybe you could run a marathon? Or join pilates classes? Or maybe you could drink more vegetable juices (these are always amazing if you want to lose more weight and gain more health).

Come up with a proper plan

When you decide to try to lose weight, it just doesn't happen overnight. You know it's a process and you are ready to go through it.

You can't just start dieting and exercising from the next day and expect to see results within a week. You have to be patient, and more importantly, you have to be organized.

Make a proper plan. Start out small, like slightly reducing unhealthy processed foods full of empty calories. Find a local, organic place where you can get fresh fruits and vegetables. Similarly, start by maybe going for a twenty-minute walk every day as exercise. Then gradually, start making your routine harder and more intense.

Start increasing the lengths of your walks. Transform your walks into jogs, and those into runs. Start hitting the gym if you want. There too, start slow and easy. Only as many pushups as you can easily muster, and smaller weights. Gradually increase the number of pushups and lifts. Start adding the quantity or mass of the weight (depending upon what machine you're using).

It's hard to stay motivated if you start too big. If you haven't exercised for ages, it's kind of hard to plan a 3-hour workout to begin with, right?

If you really find it overwhelming and can't get motivated to move your body because you don't like physical activity, simply trick your brain by following this plan: get committed to 10-minute-long home workouts every day. You can even start from 5 minutes. Why? Because this is how you can outsmart your brain.

If I tell you to go and run for 5 hours, you will probably say no. If you said yes, I'd be worried about you. However, if I tell you- hey do a 5-minute workout, my guess is that you would take action as you would associate less pain to it.

So do it now. Start jumping and dancing for 5 minutes. Do squats. Use a timer. Only 5 minutes. Sounds easy, right?

Now, go up to 10 minutes and do it twice a day. You can do it first thing in the morning to stay energized. Create a simple set of exercises you do before jumping into the shower. Do the same after work. Go from there and stick to it. Whenever you feel like: *I don't wanna do it!* Say to yourself: come on! Only 10 minutes! I am a big girl, or a big boy and I can do 10 minutes of home workout.

Easy peasy, right? So what are you waiting for? You can also design a special set of exercise for different body parts. For this strategy I recommend you have a consultation with a fitness trainer. Tell them you are on a busy schedule and ask them for specific set of routines for weight loss and wellbeing. No more excuses! There is always a way if you commit to it. Don't give up but create a plan that fits in your busy schedule.

Additionally, set milestones for yourself. That way, you'll get a particular sense of achievement when you reach one. It will increase your sense of self-esteem, motivate you to work even harder, and generally make you feel good about yourself. It will also give a sense of progress to your entire plan.

One important thing to note is that the plan you make for yourself is realistic. Do not be overly optimistic, you'll only end up disappointing yourself, and that could eventually lead you to giving up altogether. Do not be overly pessimistic either, it will just make the whole plan and your new routine seem extremely daunting, and you won't want to get started at all. Strike a balance; be realistic.

Consistency is the key. You will get there; you know you will. Rome wasn't built in a day. There is no overnight success, instead "overnight success" takes weeks and months of work to be created. You are on the right track!

Another equally important thing to note is to set the routine as per you. Just because a certain person followed a certain routine doesn't mean you have to follow it as is too. Every person is different; his/her capabilities, endurance, dedication, and body, and therefore everyone will have a different routine. Be sure to make one that suits you and your body. By this, we mean on both a physical and mental level!

Reward yourself

Losing weight is never either a small task or an easy one. It will require a considerable amount of self-sacrifice, dedication and change of routine on your part (how much exactly depends on where you're starting from and where you're planning to reach). In such a scenario, what generally happens is that one chalks out a proper routine for oneself, and then starts on it with the utmost dedication and passion. With the passage of time, one finds oneself slacking, however. A continued routine of self-sacrifice and hardship is quite difficult, after all, and to not give into dangerous desires every once in a while requires a huge amount of willpower. I'm sure we've had all those "Come on, how much harm could one ice cream cone cost?" thoughts every once in a while.

In such a scenario, it is important to come up with ways to keep yourself motivated to stick to the routine. Every time another item of junk food or high calorie food gets kicked off your list, every time the quantity of your food decreases, every time you add another to the amount you have to jog on a daily basis, every time you add another five to a number of pushups you do daily, make sure you reward yourself for it. It could be anything, provided it's not too easy to attain. That way, it won't be dangerous, and you'll have to actually work hard for it, and you'll find yourself wanting to.

Also, as mentioned before, add milestones in your overall plan. And add a reward every time you reach a milestone. For example, shedding every five pounds could be a milestone. And at every such moment, you could reward yourself by having an ice cream, maybe or have your favorite meal. There are two very important clauses to remember here, however: A) The reward shouldn't be big or elongated enough to ruin all the previous hard work, and B) The milestones shouldn't be easy or very frequent to come by! Make yourself strive and work hard for them, that way you get that sense of accomplishment too!

Also, remember that you can create delicious snacks and desserts that are nutritious and guilt-free. Always make sure you have some healthy nuts or seeds on you. You can also blend banana and some other fruits in coconut milk, sweeten it with stevia and add some spices like cinnamon or ginger. Then freeze it and you have a healthy ice-cream!

Remember to keep hydrated. Drink good quality, filtered water. I love to drink water with green powders (for example barley grass) as it helps my body hydrate and nourish itself with vital nutrients. Stop drinking sodas, instead infuse water with fruits. There are many fruit water bottles available online. Order one of them so that you always have your healthy drink with you.

When buying fruits and vegetables, wash them and chop them and store in food containers in your fridge. This is how, you will always have your healthy salads and snacks that are ready to grab. Infuse olive oil with herbs and you will have a fantastic salad dressing that is healthy and natural. Check out my recipe books for more recipe ideas. You will see that you can still keep your belly satisfied and that there is no reason to feel deprived.

Include a friend

My brother once tried to join a gym. He stuck to it for a few months, but eventually couldn't stick to it and gave up. Sometime later, he found the yearning within himself once more, but this time he approached the matter smartly. He convinced a friend of his who lives nearby to join him. Together, they've been going for two straight years now, and both of them are jacked up now!

No no, I don't mean to make you feel bad or insecure by this account. The point of sharing this little incident here is quite evident, actually. When you find yourself incapable of tackling some task yourself, don't give up or be too hard on yourself. Go to a friend for help! After all, we're neither expected nor supposed to go through all of life all alone.

Getting a friend, or a family member or anyone whose company you find pleasurable really, involved in your plan to lose weight is one of the most effective techniques to stick to your plan. The mutual support the involved parties give each other works wonders. To start with, it's always a lot more enjoyable and exciting when you start on some project, any project, with someone you know and preferably like, instead of all alone. You find yourself looking to the task, and there's also this desire to outperform yourself, in order to show your worth and the fact that it couldn't have been done without you. Additionally, when you're working on something alone and you hit a dead end, you find yourself losing hope and it's very hard to dig yourself out of this abyss. But when you have a partner with you, then he can help you or vice versa, and together you can find a solution more effectively than alone. After all, two heads are better than one!

Getting someone involved in your mission to lose weight makes the whole thing more pleasurable and enjoyable, and also provides the right kind of motivation at the exact moment when you need it the most. Two of the biggest factors to help fight demotivation and lack of hope! This is why I created by mini weight loss group through meetup.com. Like I mentioned earlier, me and two of my local friends (ladies I met online) go to the gym twice or 3 times a week. For us, it's also relaxation time. Since I work from home, I need to get out more so that I don't go crazy!

My husband wanted to lose a few extra pounds as well. We committed to it together. Now my husband did not want to go to the gym at all. He hated it. This is why we got committed to evening walks as well as to weekend excursions. Instead of staying in and watching TV and eating unhealthy food, we started spending weekends in nature. We feel so much better now. And kids love it!

Get a personal trainer

This is one of the rather extreme options, one I'd recommend as a last straw. What I would recommend is to try and hatch out a diet and exercise plan for yourself, and then try to stick it to yourself, to the best of your ability. However, if you find yourself incapable of that, and none of the above-mentioned techniques are working for you, then you can hire a personal trainer for yourself.

A personal trainer can also be sought in the scenario where you don't know how to go about the whole thing. For example, you may not know what the new diet of yours should contain. What food items you should cross off your list, which you should reduce and which you should increase. Neither are you sure about the exercises you should do, how much, how regularly etc. It is recommended then to seek a personal trainer. They are experienced in this domain, and not only that, but they are also educated. They can tell you everything perfectly, and make sure you approach the whole thing from a safe perspective. Health should always be your priority and you need to aim to lose weight in a safe way.

It may cause you to shell out a few extra bucks, but it could be well worth it. A personal trainer is actually one of the most effective techniques to not only come up with an efficient and practical plan to lose weight but which is also safe. Moreover, a personal trainer can also help you stick to the plan. That way, you can be smart and effective about the whole thing, and you'll start seeing the changes in yourself before you know it!

But remember, they will not do the job for you. They may help you get there faster by providing you with proven strategies and information that will work for you. After all, there are so many diets out there and it can be pretty overwhelming for a newbie. However, the first and final step is always yours. Be committed. You know you can do it.

Chapter 3-Why can't I stick to the plan?

The "I can't do it"

I'm sure everyone has at one point or another, faced a situation where he/she felt that it just can't be done. The odds are insurmountable, it's too difficult, and above all, the overwhelming feel that he/she just isn't capable enough.

It's okay to feel this way sometimes. We are all humans after all, and we all face tough circumstances and feel dejected and hopeless. This feeling is, in fact, one of the biggest sources of demonization in the topic being covered here as well.

When we initially start out with a weight loss plan, there's a silent battle of our wills vs the size of the task before us going on in our heads. There're motivation and passion to lose weight which wills us to go on, but there's also the daunting news of the weight loss plan; all the sacrifices we'll have to make, the huge amount of time we think it'll take, and the way we'll have to stick closely to this plan, for a few days of slacking could ruin it all. This battle just doesn't happen at the start; it's an ongoing battle; alpha vs omega, if you will, and it greatly determines whether you can stick to the plan or not.

The trick to deal with this kind of intimidation is quite simple; eliminate the intimidation altogether, or as much as you can anyway. What I mean by that is, make the task not look so daunting. Probably one of the most common phenomenon in the world is that when we're faced with a huge problem, we initially become scared and worried and start feeling the tingles of hopelessness. But when we truly dig into the problem and start understanding it, and then move on to breaking it into smaller, more manageable tasks, eventually by the end of it, we're like, "Wow, what was I so worried about?"

So as far as the weight loss plan of yours is concerned and all that it entails, break it into small tasks. Establish a proper routine for yourself. Start out small and easy, and then gradually start adding challenges. Add achievements at various points throughout the plan, and reward yourself for reaching them. Focus on the parts that you have to cope with right now, instead of what you'll have to cope with in the future. After all, if you focus on how you have to jog 2 miles tomorrow, instead of how you'll eventually have to jog 20 miles in the future, it'll be a lot easier to tackle, and will also save you from pointless worry. Follow these tips, and you'll find yourself remain motivated, and the good side shall win the battle of wills!

The "What if I fail?"

Humans are funny creatures. They have a knack for freaking out and worrying themselves crazy over things which haven't come to pass yet, and probably never will. This spectacle is so common in humans, and so relatable, that nobody really realizes how ridiculous this particular trait is.

Now I'm not saying that we're not humans, because we are. We're just trying to make the point here that it is pointless worrying over the future, but it is something we do so regularly and frequently, it comes naturally to us. And it is also one of the biggest sources of demonization and hopelessness for us.

Consider the following scenario: You start out on a weight loss plan. It consists of both a dieting plan (doctor recommended, because you want to diet the right and healthy way), and an exercise plan (you got a personal trainer because muscle pains and spasms aren't all you want, and neither do you want to find out a couple of months later that you've been doing it all wrong, and that you've just wasted all your time, effort and money so far). You stick to it regularly for quite some time, and you and the people around you have started the noticing the change in you. Everything is going well, until you start slacking and find yourself unable to stick to the plan again. Everything starts going awry; you start gaining weight again, and the people around you, your friends, family and neighbors, they all start making fun of you because of it. Pointing fingers, calling out hurtful names, and above all, mocking for how you made such a huge deal out of losing weight and went to such great lengths for it, only to end up back at square one. The humiliation and embarrassment you would have to face in such a scenario would be quite painful, no?

Bad energy!

You build all this in your head, and you grow quite scared. If you fail, that is if you can't stick to the plan, you'll have to face all the disgrace and shame that you built up in your head, yikes! And it's not exactly an easy plan to stick to, maybe you should just opt out, save it for another time...

This is what we're talking about. It's very common for people to build up all sorts of frightening and unnerving scenarios in their heads when faced with a big task, and then they just end up not doing them altogether. And here's where you have to remember that for now, it's just a hypothetical scenario in your head; it hasn't actually happened, and probably never will! You need to be brave and fight past this (baseless) fear. This is where we'll start sounding like one of those Japanese cartoons, but hey as long as it helps: You have to believe in yourself. Trust in yourself, and in your ability to carry out the weight loss plan and see it through to the end! And remember, nothing that made your skin crawl with both intimidation and anticipation isn't worth doing anyway.

In fact, this is one of those sources of demoralization that you can turn around and use in a positive way too. Start on your weight loss plan, stick to it firmly, and use this scenario you've imagined as a means of intimidation, to scare you not out of ditching the plan altogether, but rather to stick to it all the firmly and dedicatedly!

Focus. Focus will help. If you decide to focus on "I will fail", it will be a really painful journey and it may end up in tears. But the good news is that you can also focus on the positive. You can choose to focus on successful weight loss stories. I mean- people do it. Everyone can lose weight. This is why you can do it too. Humans can lose weight, and you are a human, right? All your "what if I fail" problems are imaginary. Your brain is trying to protect you from leaving your comfort zone. Outsmart it by being brave!

The "I don't want to do it"

I have a degree in Computer Science (I know it's strange for a female), and one phenomenon that I observed throughout my four years in university was one that amused me greatly, but also taught me a very important principle of life. You see, most of the students in the same program, as I was, were people who were not really interested in the domain. They were students who couldn't get enrolled in a better university, or in the program of their choice, and ultimately chose Computer Science in this university. And all four years, they were a picture of misery. They struggled through all the assignments, they barely gave any quizzes, they tried to cram a semester's worth of syllabus in one night before the final, and they just scraped through all the courses, with the utmost difficulty. This wasn't because they were dumb, or that the course load was too much or the studies too tough for them. No, it was because they simply didn't put in an effort. And why not? Because the domain, and all that it entailed wasn't of their interest.

Man is known all too well for not putting in enough, or the required amount, of effort in something which doesn't catch his fancy. It's a universal rule: anything we like and are passionate about, we'll do it excitedly, we'll want to do it, and we'll naturally, perhaps even unconsciously, put a lot of effort into it. Contrary to when something fails to garner out curiosity and passion, and we find ourselves doing it with more of 'because we have to' air; in the case of which, we barely put any effort into it.

So before opting for a diet plan, make sure you are clear on several things. One of the most important things would be, why are you going for a weight loss plan? What are the stakes, and the risks involved? What happens if you don't opt for this plan? What happens if you don't manage to see it through to the end? Make sure you have your facts straight regarding all that will be required, and above all, the reason that you're going for it. For if you don't, then halfway through or perhaps even much sooner, you'll find yourself wanting to give up, or barely sticking to the plan just because you have to. And if those are the reasons you're sticking to the plan, then trust me, you won't be able to stick to it for much longer!

Make sure to do your homework. Come up with at least 5 reasons why you want to lose weight.

Ask yourself a few questions:

- How will my health change if I lose weight? And what will happen if I don't lose weight?
- How will my social life change if I lose weight? And how what will happen if I don't achieve my goal?
- How will my professional life change if I lose weight? And what will happen if I don't take action and keep neglecting my weight and my health?

My situation was that I wanted to become a holistic nutritionist. I have always had a passion for food and cooking but the problem was that I did not know how to cook healthy and nutritious meals. This is why, I wanted to study nutrition and healthy diets. I needed education. Then, I knew I wanted to help other people lose weight and I used it as my motivator.

Imagine you want to hire a wealth or success coach. Would you hire a success coach who is broke and living with their parents? Probably not. You would want to hire someone who is wealthy and successful, right? We always want coaches and mentors with visible results.

Would you hire a weight loss coach who is overweight? Of course not. This is how Kira managed to stay motivated.

I used pain as my motivator as well. But I also had other motivators and I had a clearly defined vision for my health and family life.

If your situation somehow dictates that you have to lose weight but you're not particularly excited about, or you're not very passionate about it and aren't exactly looking forward to the process, then you can make it interesting! Add small tweaks and adjustments to your routine here and there which makes it more fun, interesting, and ultimately, something to look forward to! Some ideas we can give here are involving a friend, putting on your favorite music while working out, rewarding yourself with a treat after every week or month, and so on. Spice things up, make them fun! Create a positive vision board, it will help you stay focused and grounded.

The "What if I succeed?"

This may sound rather strange at first, and we can't blame you for that. After all, who really would be afraid of success? Isn't that what everyone is striving for?

You would, of course, be right, and can't be blamed for this confusion. Everyone is, everywhere, in every waking moment, striving for some sort of success of one form or another, in one form or another. Be we chasing after money, or some sort of self-satisfaction, or to impress the people around us, or some personal goal; all of these are fronts for the same underlying purpose; to succeed. And when we manage to achieve one or more of these goals, the realization that we succeeded gives us a feeling of accomplishment and achievement, along with the practical purpose of the goal(s).

However, succeeding in achieving a goal also has a downside as well. When we achieve some form of success, then underneath all the euphoria and celebrations of any, we have this sinking feeling that now that we achieved this particular goal, people will expect more from us. This can happen in all walks of life. If you are a student and got good marks in the mid-terms, your parents will expect even better from you in the finals. If you are an employee and you did a good job on the project which was assigned to you, your boss will appreciate and congratulate you, but he/she will also expect the same amount and quality of effort from you in all future projects as well, if not more. If you get your wife a silver necklace for her birthday, she will love it – and you for it – but she may expect a gold one on her next birthday.

And of course, if you go on a weight loss plan and achieve a certain amount of success, people will be amazed and happy for you, but they will also expect you to go further, and lose even more weight, grow even fitter. You can use it as your motivator as well but...

The fact that people's expectations from you will always grow every time you achieve something, and eventually there will come a time when you won't be able to meet them, is quite a disheartening one.

The key here is to have your goals set out from the very beginning and to also know your capabilities and limits, and proceed accordingly. This way, you'll know how to proceed and when to stop.

The "It wasn't supposed to be this hard"

Yet another source of discouragement and loss of hope while going through a weight loss plan occurs when you don't seem to meet your goals as well as you had thought you would. For example, you may have planned a proper schedule for yourself spanning over several weeks or months, but you were unconsciously overly optimistic about the results, and the pace at which you would start seeing them. And a few weeks into the plan, you realize that you're falling short of all the milestones you'd set for yourself. This will lead to frustration, eventually if not immediately, and finally you'll give up on the new routine altogether.

The opposite of this scenario is also a possibility. Suppose that while setting the plan for yourself, you, again unconsciously, do just the contrary: become overly pessimistic. The routine you end up with is far too long and arduous, because you vastly underestimated the amount of time, energy, and sacrifices you'll have to invest. This routine will only appear extremely daunting and scary, and chances are, you'll never find the energy to actually embark on it. You'll just find yourself making excuses to avoid it, and making fruitless pledges to 'start tomorrow instead', and eventually you'll come to terms with the fact that this plan is something that's just too tough for you, and you can't do it, so might as well forget about it altogether.

The solution here is to be neither optimistic, not pessimistic while making the weight loss plan for yourself, but just the right mix of both, accompanied of course by a high dosage of a realistic approach. Remember to approach the weight loss process with curiosity. Try to see it as a healthy experiment. It's all about being consistent. If you think that weight loss and health are not for you, you are wrong. You deserve vibrant health and the body you want. This is why you need to create your health foundation. Whenever having a bad day, say to yourself:

"It's not about weight loss. I am going to focus on health"

Then try to come up with a healthy recipe or activity. While it's important to have your weight loss goals, it's also important to remember not too get too obsessed about them. If you constantly think about your weight, you will end up burned out. It's much easier to follow a simple "I wanna be healthy" plan that is less stressful. As long as you focus on healthy foods and move your body, you will start losing weight. Remember that physical and emotional healthy should never be the price of your weight loss success.

Chapter 4-No Guilt Trips – What to do when you get off track

Let yourself off easy!

There are different kinds of people in the world; no two are ever the same. While we could come up with virtually infinite measures on the basis of which we could differentiate people, the one we'll use here is how people cope with disappointment and failure.

It is natural to feel sad, dejected, as well as a major lack of help and drop in self-esteem when one experiences failure. It doesn't really matter what a person failed in, really. Any kind of failure can seriously bring a person down, and can transform them from the life of the party, to the dead body in the coffin. Okay, that example doesn't make a lot of sense, if any, but we hope that it illustrates our point.

Different people react differently to different situations. If something good happens like say, the national football team won the world cup: Some people would be overjoyed and would jump and scream in joy, and talk about it for the next whole month. Some people would be happy about it, but not overly expressive. And some people would be totally indifferent!

Likewise, people react differently to sad or heartbreaking situations as well. At the death of a loved one, some people cry their eyes out, while others just remain silent and aloof. Everyone reacts differently to different situations, even though down inside they're all experiencing the same emotion.

When it comes to dealing with failures, there are usually two kinds of people. There are those who don't let the disappointment get to them, and get back on track, or choose a change of direction. While others would go into depression and despair, and won't feel like taking up the challenge, or any other for that matter, for a long time, if at all. Out of these two, the type of person you are when faced with failure depends upon the magnitude of the task you're faced with.

In the case of going off track of a weight loss plan, the sense of failure is usually very high. After all, it was no small project. You motivated yourself enough to start on it, you hatched out a proper schedule for yourself, and you stuck to it regularly for a certain amount of time… Until you eventually started slacking, and eventually went off track. Because of this, the dejection felt at the loss of failing to see the plan through to the end is usually very high, and people don't really feel like getting back on the bandwagon for a really long time, if ever.

The key here is to be easy on yourself. Do not let the loss get to you. It is okay to slack and get off track. You have to realize that you're not the only one; there are tons of people in the world who faced the same failure as you. It's not the end of the world, and more importantly, just because you slacked here does not mean it's over. No, whether it is over or not depends on what you do next. Do you get back to pursuing the weight loss plan with perhaps even more vigor? Or do you remain slouched on your couch, eating popcorn, and letting defeat get to you, actually marking it as one?

Do not be too hard on yourself. Convert your regret into a source of fueling your passion and vigor, and get back on track with even more determination! You'll see it through this time.

Jog your memory, remember the purpose!

Sometimes it happens that you embark on a certain journey with a purpose; it could be anything, really. For example, you could find yourself going on a world tour with the purpose of meeting new people, introducing yourself to new cultures and traditions, and increase your knowledge of the world and its people. Or, you could take a leave from office, and use the time to experiment with your other interests or passions. See if they can get you anywhere; after all, there's no harm in trying, right? But halfway or so through this personal journey, people sometimes forget the true purpose of the journey, the reason behind it. And when that happens, they just quit altogether.

Why do they quit? Well you see, the sense of purpose is very strong and important whenever anyone sets out to do something. If you set out to get good grades, it's because you want to make your parents happy, or secure your future. If you put in extra hours at work, it's so that you get noticed by your boss, or to increase your chances of getting a promotion. But when there's no purpose, then you just don't feel like pursuing the journey at all. A perfect example of this would be the students who are enrolled in a program they have absolutely zero interest in. A student who's very passionate about and extremely good in arts, enrolled in an Electrical Engineering program would have absolutely no sense of purpose in getting good grades or trying to learn something in the program, because he does not want to be an Electrical Engineer! He wants, and plans, to be an artist when he grows up, and that is what his profession will be. So he does not pursue the Electrical Engineering degree because there's no purpose of him doing so!

This will all get relative now, I swear. You see, when you get off track while pursuing a weight loss plan, one of the most effective techniques for getting back on track is to remind yourself of the purpose. Why did you set out on this journey in the first place? What was the reason which prompted you to do something about it, and get so far? At times, reminding yourself of the purpose is just the kick you need to get back on track!

Figure out the problem(s)

One of the most important things to do when you find yourself having gotten sidetracked from a weight loss plan, or any other project for that matter, is to figure out where you went wrong. What were the problems? What were the hard parts? Why were you not able to pursue your goals? What created hindrances, what obstacles did you face?

Sometimes, instead of giving in to depression and misery, it helps you analyze the whole thing critically. How did you start, how far did you get, when did it start becoming difficult, at what point did you start slacking, what were the reasons? Once you identify the problems, your mind will automatically start figuring out solutions. This way, you'll be approaching the problem anew, but with a very important tool in your arsenal: experience. More than that, having figured out the problems and then pursuing the plan once more will also give you a greater sense of confidence than you did when you initially started. Because now, you know what problems you can and will run into, and how to deal with them, get past them, and move on.

Set small scale goals for yourself

After months of your wife or husband (or kids) being continuously on your case to get up from the couch, go outside and take a walk, in order to lose some of the fat, you finally give in. Your determination with your spouse's even more determined nagging now that he/she sees it working, you hatch out a weight loss plan (with their help, God bless them). You start out on a diet and exercise program, stick to it religiously for quite some time... Until your spouse stops nagging you. Consequently, you lose your biggest source of motivation, and you find yourself going back to your couch potato routine.

Why? Because you did not work with your inner motivation. You focused on external motivation. In other words- you did not learn how to motivate yourself.

Seeing the danger approaching, your spouse once more starts getting on your case, but now it seems so difficult. You tried once; it didn't work out, what are the chances of it working another time? Plus, the starting is always the hardest part, as you know all too well now, and you really don't want to go through all the initial stages again!

When faced with such a situation (with or without the nagging spouse), it can be hard to convince yourself to get back on track, particularly because you'll have to go through the preliminary stages once more, and those are the worst. What you can do here is to start out slow; as slow as you need to be in order to get comfortable with the idea of starting out on the routine once more. Don't assume that just because you reached a certain point in the weight loss plan, you'll have to start from exactly that point when you restart, that can actually be very intimidating! No, start out slow, increase your tempo gradually, and you shall be good to go.

Honesty time – what are my weaknesses?

Before getting back on track with the weight loss program, one of the most important things to do is to sit you down, and have some honest time with yourself. What honest time refers to here is you evaluating your progress, up till the point where you went awry, and not figuring out what went wrong, but rather, why.

In other words, you don't focus on what occurred which led you off track. Focus on the reason behind it. It is important to know your weak areas. You should know your limitations, the pace at which you can progress, and your breaking point. It may be hard since you'll have to be completely true with yourself and in the process, you'll probably end up realizing quite a few things about yourself that you never wanted to, and which might hit you like a ton of bricks. But it is important. Because when you get back on track with the weight loss plan, you don't just blatantly embark on it once more with exactly the same plan as before!

You have to be smart about the whole thing when you're restarting your weight loss program. With all the knowledge gained about your weaknesses, limitations, and breaking points, you can now revise your schedule and plan. You can, and should, modify it to suit you and your body, and make sure it accounts for your weaknesses. That way, when you actually restart, you won't be making the same mistakes again. You'll be learning from them, and making sure they don't occur in the future!

Before you go, I'd like to remind you that there is a free, complimentary eBook (pdf format) waiting for you:

Download link:

http://detox.kiraglutenfreerecipes.com

Conclusion

And there you have it, folks! A complete, all-in-one guide that anybody looking to lose weight at any point in time will need. As we stated in the beginning, the physical aspect of a weight loss plan is only half the game. The other mental half, which basically dictates how well you can stick to the plan and focuses on gaining motivation to do so, is just as important, yet somehow comparatively less focused on everywhere.

So remember, the next time (and the very last time) you embark on a weight loss plan, ensure to keep these motivational tips handy! And if you find yourself getting off track, make yourself understand that it's not the end of the world – or your plan, for that matter. You can still get back on track, and continue on and eventually succeed in your mission to become the next major athlete or model!

To post an honest review

One more thing… If you have received any value from this book, can you please rank it and post a short review? It only takes a few seconds really and it would really make my day. It's you I am writing for and your opinion is always much appreciated. In order to do so;

1. Log into your account
2. Search for my book on Amazon or check your orders/ or go to my author page at:

http://amazon.com/author/kira-novac

3. Click on a book you have read, then click on "reviews" and "create your review".

Please let me know your favorite motivational tip you learned from this book.

I would love to hear from you!

If you happen to have any questions or doubts about this book, please e-mail me at:

kira.novac@kiraglutenfreerecipes.com

I am here to help!

Recommended FREE eBook

Book Link:

http://bit.ly/juicing-diet-book

FOR MORE HEALTH BOOKS (KINDLE & PAPERBACK) BY KIRA NOVAC PLEASE VISIT:

www.kiraglutenfreerecipes.com/books

Thank you for taking an interest in my work,

Kira and Holistic Wellness Books

HOLISTIC WELLNESS & HEALTH BOOKS

If you are interested in health, wellness, spirituality and personal development, visit our page and be the first one to know about free and 0.99 eBooks:

www.HolisticWellnessBooks.com

www.ingramcontent.com/pod-product-compliance
Lightning Source LLC
Chambersburg PA
CBHW072207100526
44589CB00015B/2411